# THE SEMINOLE

## A TRUE BOOK®

by
**Stefanie Takacs**

**Children's Press®**
A Division of Scholastic Inc.

New York  Toronto  London  Auckland  Sydney
Mexico City  New Delhi  Hong Kong
Danbury, Connecticut

A Seminole woman holding up a strip of patchwork

Reading Consultant
**Jeanne Clidas, Ph.D.**
*National Reading Consultant
and Professor of Reading,
SUNY Brockport*

Content Consultant
**Patsy West**
*Executive Director,
Seminole/Miccosukee
Photographic Archive*

Library of Congress Cataloging-in-Publication Data

Takacs, Stefanie.
   The Seminole / by Stefanie Takacs.— 1st American ed.
      p. cm.  —  (A true book)
   Includes bibliographical references and index.
Contents: The beginnings of new tribe — Settling into a new land —
Daily life in the 1800s — Culture and customs — Years of struggle —
The Seminole today.
   ISBN 0-516-22781-5 (lib. bdg.)    0-516-27908-4 (pbk.)
   1. Seminole Indians—Juvenile literature. [1. Seminole Indians. 2.
Indians of North America—Oklahoma. 3. Indians of North America—
Southern States.] I. Title. II. Series.
E99.S28T35 2003
975.9004'973—dc21
                                                         2003004543

1 2 3 4 5 6 7 8 9 10 R 12 11 10 09 08 07 06 05 04 03

# Contents

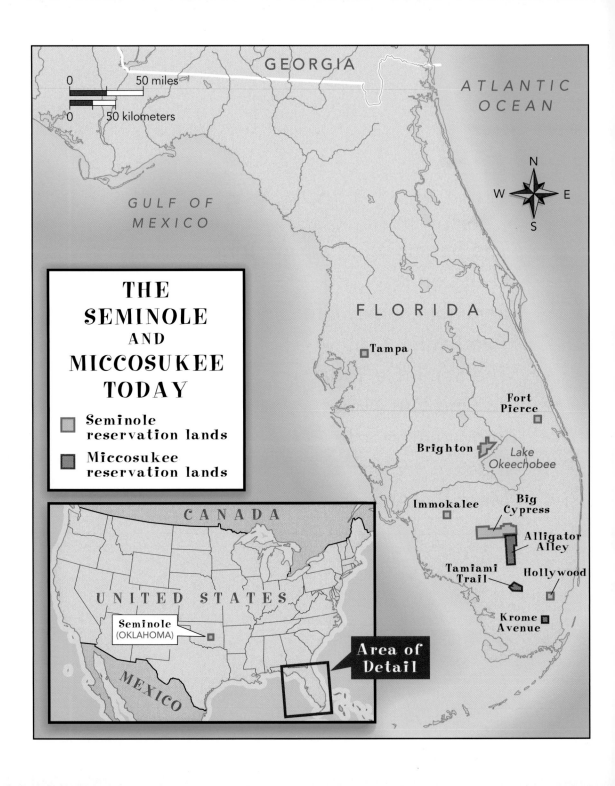

GEORGIA

ATLANTIC OCEAN

0 — 50 miles

0 — 50 kilometers

GULF OF MEXICO

N
W · E
S

FLORIDA

Tampa

Fort Pierce

Brighton · Lake Okeechobee

## THE SEMINOLE AND MICCOSUKEE TODAY

Seminole reservation lands

Miccosukee reservation lands

Immokalee

Big Cypress

Alligator Alley

Tamiami Trail

Hollywood

Krome Avenue

CANADA

UNITED STATES

Seminole (OKLAHOMA)

MEXICO

Area of Detail

# The Beginning of a New Tribe

For thousands of years, American Indians had lived on the **continent** of North America. In the 1700s, many different groups moved into what is now northern Florida. People who European settlers called "Creeks" fled to Florida from Georgia and Alabama. There they joined with people of the Yamasee, Mikisuki, Apalachee, and Yuchi tribes.

The Indians who took **refuge** in Florida wanted to put distance between them- selves and European settlers. These settlers were steadily moving into what is now the southeastern part of the United States. As they did, they took over the lands of American Indian peoples.

Creek Indians (above) lived in Georgia and Alabama. Some of these people moved to Florida and became part of the Seminole tribe.

The Indians living in Florida called themselves *istî siminolî* or *yat'siminolî*. They became known as the "Seminole."

Runaway black slaves who fled to Florida formed communities near the Seminole.

The Seminole were soon joined by African slaves who had escaped from American **plantations.** The ex-slaves became known as "Black Seminoles." They lived in separate communities near the Indians. Though some of these people became the Seminoles' slaves, they were treated with respect. The Black Seminoles used their knowledge of farming to help the Seminole. They tended their fields and cattle. They received protection from the Seminole in exchange for giving the Seminole a portion of their crops. They all enjoyed living in peace.

Unfortunately, peaceful times did not last. Angry slave owners came down into Florida to hunt for those who had escaped. Sometimes, they burned entire Seminole villages as they looked for the runaway slaves and Seminole cattle. The Seminole fought back to protect their slaves, cattle, and families. This series of conflicts across the Florida-Georgia border started the First Seminole War (1814–1818).

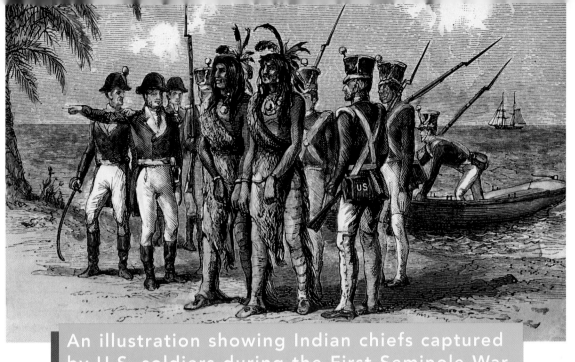

An illustration showing Indian chiefs captured by U.S. soldiers during the First Seminole War

In 1821, Florida became an official territory of the United States. More settlers began moving south. Naturally, they wanted all the good farmland for themselves. The Seminole were in their way.

In 1830, the United States signed the Indian Removal Act. The new law said that all the Indian tribes on the East Coast had to move to Oklahoma. The United States promised the Indian tribes good land and a safe place to live. However, the government had broken its promises before. The Indians did not trust them.

The Seminole people would not leave for Oklahoma. Instead, they stayed and fought against the U.S. Army.

The Second Seminole War
(1835–1842) was the bloodiest
and most costly of all Indian wars.
Just as in the first war, there was
no winner. The Seminole refused
to surrender and the United States

A Seminole attack on a U.S. fort
during the Second Seminole War

grew weary of fighting. The government tried other ways to convince the Seminole to leave.

Eventually, most of the Seminole were removed to Oklahoma along with the Cherokee, the Chickasaw, the Choctaw, and the Creek. There, they became known as the "Five Civilized Tribes."

Fewer than three hundred Seminole remained in Florida. More conflicts with settlers led to the Third Seminole War (1855–1858). Again, there was no winner. The Seminole would not surrender.

Those Seminole who remained in Florida after the Third Seminole War moved deep into the Florida Everglades.

They simply moved further south—deep into the swamp-land of the Florida Everglades.

# Osceola and Abiaka

During the Seminole Wars, two famous men inspired the tribe to keep fighting for their freedom.

Osceola was a great Seminole warrior who fought passionately against U.S. forces. He was also a skillful **orator**. In 1837, Osceola traveled to meet with United States military leaders. Although they had promised peace, U.S. soldiers surrounded Osceola. They threw him into prison, where he later died.

Osceola

Some say Abiaka, also known as Sam Jones, was even more powerful than Osceola. This medicine man stirred up the Seminole warriors with his speeches. His religious ceremonies prepared them for war. Abiaka urged his people: "Never surrender!"

# Living on the Land

Every member of the Seminole tribe is born into a clan, or family group. Children belong to their mother's clan. At one time, there were more than twenty Seminole clans in Florida. Fourteen clans moved to Oklahoma. Eight remained in Florida. The Panther, Bird,

Seminole children are born into the clan of their mother.

Bear, Deer, Wind, Big Town, Snake, and Otter are the Florida Seminole clans.

For many years, the clans lived in villages in the southern part of the Florida **peninsula.**

They kept their homes simple—wooden frames made of cypress logs with roofs of **palmetto** leaves. These "chickees" had no walls and no furniture. The family slept on the wooden platform that covered the floor.

A chickee

Everyone shared the respon-sibility of providing food for the village. Members of the community took turns working on the village farm. Each family also had a smaller garden in which to grow their own food. They grew vegetables such as corn, beans, pumpkins, and squash. They hunted for deer, bear, and **manatees.** They caught fish and turtles, and kept **domesticated** hogs. All of the food was brought to the community "cooking chickee." Everyone ate there together.

Traditional Seminole foods, including corn, beans, pumpkins, and squash (below), were prepared in a cooking chickee (bottom). This photo (right) from the early 1900s shows Seminole women pounding corn to make a traditional food called *sofkee.*

# Seminole Family Life

When a Seminole boy became a man, he was given a new name. He could sit at the council fire with the other men and meet with tribal elders. Seminole men had certain responsibilities in their community. They built the chickees. They worked on the village farm.

This Seminole man is making a cypress canoe the same way his people have done for generations.

The men hunted for food in the forests, swamps, rivers, and streams. They carved out tree trunks to make canoes for fishing and travel.

These photographs show how Seminole people dressed in the late 1800s.

Seminole women prepared all meals. They did farm work with the men, tended their hogs, cared for their young children, and made clothing.

Young girls began wearing neck-laces of large beads at an early age—adding more and more as they reached adulthood. In the 1800s, Seminole women wore floor-length skirts and short blouses trimmed with a ruffle.

An explorer who visited the Everglades in the 1890s noted that there was a sewing machine in every Seminole camp. Over time, the use of the sewing machine brought about a change in Seminole clothing style. By the 1920s, Seminole

Seminole women have been creating beautiful patchwork clothing since the early 1900s.

women had begun to create the bright, colorful patchwork clothing for which the Seminole are famous.

# Two Faiths

Today, the Seminole people have two religions: traditional beliefs and Christianity. Both faiths are based on a belief in a Creator. The traditional religion includes special ceremonies for worship and thanksgiving.

Each spring, the Seminole New Year begins with the

This drawing shows people participating in the Green Corn Dance.

Green Corn Dance. This spiritual celebration lasts for four days. It includes important annual ceremonies—and hours and hours of social or "stomp" dancing.

# The Stick Ball Game

**D**uring the Green Corn Dance, people take part in a social ceremonial game called the stick ball game. It is played with a tall pole or tree, racquets, and a ball about the size of a tennis ball.

A mark is placed about 10 feet (3 m) down from the top of the pole. Players are divided into two teams. The object is to toss the ball up and hit the top of the pole. Men use racquets to move the ball  and women use their hands.

Teams receive 4 points for hitting the top of the pole and 2 points for hitting the part of the pole between the top of the pole and the mark. The first team to reach a pre-set number of points wins.

Men and women weave in and out, back and forth in single file. The women wear "shakers" attached to their ankles. A medicine man leads the people in chanting.

In the 1840s, Christian missionaries began sharing their faith with the Seminole people of Oklahoma. Hundreds of tribal members decided to become Christians themselves. In 1907, a group of Seminole Christians left Oklahoma. They traveled to share their beliefs with the

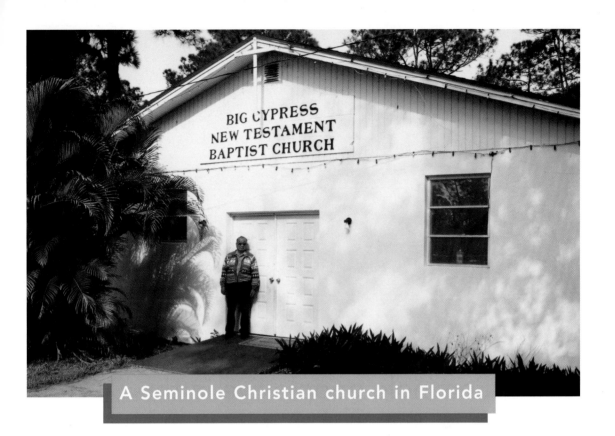

A Seminole Christian church in Florida

Seminole in Florida. Over time, the Christian faith spread. Today, Christianity is an important part of Seminole life. There are several active Christian churches among the Seminole people today.

# The Seminole Today

More than sixteen thousand Seminole people live in the United States today. The Seminole Nation of Oklahoma lists over twelve thousand tribal members—most of whom live in or around Seminole County, Oklahoma. The Seminole Tribe of Florida

An Oklahoma Seminole woman and her children wearing traditional clothing for a festival (right) and Seminole children playing on the Brighton Reservation in Florida (below)

has more than three thousand members who live on six major **reservations** across the state.

In 1934, the United States finally recognized the right of American Indians to govern themselves. In response, the Oklahoma Seminole reorganized their tribal government in the mid-1930s. The Florida Seminole formed an organized government in 1957. They wrote a **constitution** and began officially calling themselves the Seminole Tribe of Florida.

Under their two tribal governments, the Seminole elect leaders to represent them at

Betty Mae Jumper was the first female chairman of the Florida Seminole council.

tribal councils. In Oklahoma, the person who has been elected as the head of the General Council is called the "chief." In Florida, the top Seminole leader is called the "chairman."

A Miccosukee woman swinging a child in a hammock

In 1962, a group of Indians in southern Florida who were culturally related to the Seminole decided to organize a tribe of their own. They named themselves the Miccosukee Tribe of Indians of Florida. Since then, the Seminole and Miccosukee have been recognized as two separate tribes of Florida Indians. Today, the Miccosukee Tribe has about five hundred members.

The two Seminole Tribes run many different kinds of businesses. They own hotels and restaurants. They operate large farms that produce corn and citrus fruit. The Florida

A Seminole cattle farm in Florida

Seminole breed cattle, and the Oklahoma Seminole breed horses. In Florida, tribal members re-create traditional arts and crafts and patchwork clothing. These items are sold at museums and tourist attractions.

The Seminole bring tourist dollars into their communities by selling such traditional crafts as beaded necklaces (left) and sweetgrass baskets (below). A few Seminole and Miccosukee men "wrestle" alligators to entertain tourists (bottom).

Pictured here is a Seminole rodeo on the Hollywood Reservation in Florida.

Thousands of people gather each year at Seminole and Miccosukee fairs in Oklahoma and Florida. At these festivals, tribal members dress in traditional costumes. They sing old songs and tell old stories. They perform ceremonial dances. Artists display their crafts. Members participate in parades, contests, and rodeos. It is a time to celebrate their culture and history—the Seminole and Miccosukee way of life.

Today, most Seminole and Miccosukee wear modern clothing. They work in a variety of

An employee at a Seminole-owned aircraft company in Fort Pierce, Florida

jobs and professions. They live in houses and apartment buildings. They drive their cars to work. Websites and online groups help members of the tribe connect with one another. Although much has changed, the Seminole and Miccosukee remain proud of their people and their past.

A man leading a traditional stomp dance at a Seminole cultural festival

# To Find Out More

Here are some additional resources to help you learn more about the Seminole:

 **Books**

Gaines, Richard M. **The Seminole.** ABDO Publishing Company, 2000.

Jumper, Betty Mae. **Legends of the Seminoles.** Pineapple Press, 1998.

Kavasch, E. Barrie. **Seminole Children and Elders Talk Together.** Rosen Publishing, 1999.

Koslow, Philip. **The Seminole Indians.** Chelsea House, 1994.

Lund, Bill. **Seminole Indians.** Bridgestone Books, 1997.

Sneve, Virginia Driving Hawk. **The Seminoles.** Holiday House, 1994.

Sonneborn, Liz. **The Seminole.** Franklin Watts, 2002.

West, Patsy. **The Seminole and Miccosukee Tribes of Southern Florida.** Arcadia Publishers, 2002.

## Organizations and Online Sites

**Ah-Tah-Thi-Ki Museum**
HC-61 Box 21-A
Clewiston, FL 33440
*http://www.seminoletribe.
com/museum/*

In the Seminole language, Ah-Tah-Thi-Ki means "to learn." This museum, located on the Big Cypress Reservation, teaches about Seminole culture and history through exhibits, nature trails, and a living village.

**Seminole Nation of Oklahoma Museum**
524 South Wewoka Ave.
Wewoka, OK 74884
*http://www.lasr.net/leisure/
oklahoma/seminole/
wewoka/att1.html*

Visit this site to learn about the Seminole Nation of Oklahoma Museum.

**The Seminole Nation of Oklahoma**
*http://www.cowboy.net/
native/seminole/index.html*

This official site of the Seminole Nation of Oklahoma features brief articles on its history, as well as historical and modern photographs.

**The Seminole Tribe of Florida**
*http://www.seminoletribe.
com*

This official site of the Florida Seminole provides all kinds of information about Seminole culture and history—from photos to legends to recipes.

**Florida Kids Page**
*http://dhr.dos.state.fl.us/kids/*

This is the official kids site for the history of the State of Florida.

**Oklahoma Indian Affairs Commission**
*http://www.oiac.state.ok.us/
factfigures.html*

Check out this official Oklahoma Indian Affairs Commission website for kids.

45

# Important Words

*constitution* the laws and principles set up to govern a nation

*continent* one of the major land areas of the Earth

*domesticated* tamed, not wild

*manatees* sea mammals with flippers and broad flat tails that live off the coast of Florida and in the Gulf of Mexico

*orator* speaker

*palmetto* type of palm tree having crowns of fan-shaped leaves

*peninsula* piece of land nearly surrounded by water

*plantations* large farms, often run by the work of slaves

*refuge* shelter or protection from danger

*reservations* areas of land set aside for Indian groups by the U.S. government

# Meet the Author

Stefanie Takacs has worked in social services, youth education and programming, and educational publishing. She has written numerous educational books on reading-test preparation and Native American peoples. Stefanie holds a bachelor's degree in liberal arts and a master's degree in educational psychology.

Experiencing new cultures is part of Stefanie's life. She has lived in Africa, South America, and the United States. She has also traveled extensively through the United Kingdom and Europe. These days Stefanie can be found in the Bronx, New York, or in the Litchfield Hills of Connecticut, where she enjoys gardening, reading, writing, running, painting and drawing, and being with her family.

Photographs © 2003: Art Resource, NY/National Museum of American Art, Washington DC: 16; Corbis Images: 36 (Patrick Ward), 39 bottom left (Nik Wheeler); Historical Museum of Southern Florida, Ralph Munroe Collection: 24 right, 24 left; Nativestock.com/Marilynn "Angel" Wynn: cover, 1, 13, 19, 21 bottom, 21 top left, 21 top right, 28, 29, 38, 39 right, 39 top left, 40, 42, 43; North Wind Picture Archives: 7, 8, 11; Oklahoma Historical Society, Archives and Manuscripts Division: 33 top, 35; Raymond Bial: 26; Silver Image/John J. Lopinot: 23, 33 bottom; Stock Boston: 15 (Mark C. Burnett), 2 (Willie L. Hill Jr.); Superstock, Inc.: 18; The Seminole Tribune, Seminole Communications/Pete Gallagher: 31. Map by Bob Italiano.

# Index